For _____
builders everywhere

Copyright © 1993 by Bert Kitchen

All rights reserved.

First U.S. edition 1993
Published in Great Britain in 1993
by Walker Books Ltd., London.

Library of Congress Cataloging-in-Publication Data

Kitchen, Bert.
And so they build / by Bert Kitchen.—
1st U.S. ed.

Summary: Describes, in text and illustrations,
twelve animal architects and why and how they
build their unusual structures.
ISBN 1-56402-217-X
1. Animals—Habitations—Juvenile literature.
2. Parental behavior in animals—Juvenile literature.
[1. Animals—Habitations.   2. Animals—Habits and
behavior.]   I. Title.
QL756.K57   1993
591.56'4 — dc20   92-54403

10 9 8 7 6 5 4 3 2 1

Printed in Singapore

The pictures in this book were
done in watercolors and gouache.

Candlewick Press
2067 Massachusetts Avenue
Cambridge, Massachusetts 02140

AND SO THEY BUILD

BY BERT KITCHEN

CANDLEWICK PRESS

CAMBRIDGE, MASSACHUSETTS

A male satin bowerbird is looking for a mate and so he builds...

Satin bowerbirds live in the rainforests of eastern Australia. When the male is ready to attract a mate, he clears a site in dappled sunlight and shade on the forest floor. Then he builds a bower of sticks and decorates the ground with whatever bright objects he can find — parrot feathers, shells, flowers, fruits, leaves, and even scraps of cloth. Most of the objects are blue, and the bowerbird often paints the inside walls with the blue juice of berries, too. He carpets the open end of his bower with twigs, making a stage on which he will perform his courtship dance. If his efforts attract a female satin bowerbird, she will enter his bower and wait inside to mate with him. Then the two birds will desert the bower for a nest built by the female in a tree nearby.

Mallee fowl are preparing for a brood and so they build...

Mallee fowl live in the arid eucalyptus woodlands of Australia. In winter the male mallee fowl will dig a pit about three feet deep and heap it high with vegetation. Once it has been dampened by the winter rains, he covers it with a mound of sand to rot and build up heat. It takes about four months for the inside of the mound to heat up to 90°F, and throughout this period he keeps a constant check on its temperature, using his tongue as a thermometer. When the mound is warm enough, he makes holes for his mate to lay her eggs in. This she does over the course of several months, laying one egg every few days and covering it up again afterward.

For the time it takes the eggs to hatch, the male bird continues to monitor the heat of the mound, adding or removing sand as necessary.

Cubiterme termites are in danger of getting drenched and so they build...

Cubiterme termites are often called white ants, but are actually more closely related to cockroaches. Some cubitermes, living in parts of West Africa where there is heavy rainfall, have developed an ingenious way of keeping their nests dry.

The workers of a colony build one or more columns out of tiny pellets of soil cemented together with saliva. The building begins below ground and extends above to a height of around eighteen inches. Inside is an intricate system of living chambers, brood cells, food storage areas, and vents for controlling the temperature.

The final touch is exceptional. Each column is capped with an umbrella-shaped roof, which serves to divert torrential rain and protect the termites living below.

A pregnant harvest mouse will soon have a family and so she builds...

This tiny mouse is found in areas ranging from Britain to Japan. Before her babies are born, the female mouse weaves a nest around a group of upright, growing stalks in a cultivated field, using long leaves still attached to the plants to form the basic shape. She weaves the walls with blades of grass, which she first shreds lengthways into manageable strands with her sharp teeth, and lines the nest with shorter shredded blades of grass and other soft plants.

Warm, comfortable, and safely suspended above ground — growing higher and higher as the stalks to which it is attached grow — this perfect nest for baby mice takes their mother just five to ten hours to build.

Swallows are ready to breed and so they build...

Swallows fly almost everywhere in the world apart from the Arctic and Antarctic, though they winter exclusively in the Southern Hemisphere. They normally build their nests on a sheltered ledge or beam — perhaps inside a barn. They begin by plastering mud from a nearby pond or stream onto the wall above the ledge, then build up their nest in semicircular layers of mudballs, adding grass and straw for extra strength.

It may take as many as a thousand mouthfuls of mud, carried back one by one, to build a nest.

Swallows often return to the same place each year, repairing their nests with fresh mud and straw.

A paper wasp is about to start her colony and so she builds...

The paper wasp is found in North America, Europe, and North Africa.
Before she lays her eggs, the female wasp uses her powerful jaws to scrape wood from any post, fence, or beam that she can find. She adds her saliva to the wood to create a unique paper mixture.

Now she begins to build her nest, which hangs from a plant stem, stone, or board.
It takes the form of a comb made up of hexagonal cells, in each of which she lays one egg, effectively gluing it to the base to keep it from falling out. The comb has no cover, but it is very well insulated. Inside their snug cells the eggs will develop into larvae and finally into adult wasps.

A tailorbird will be safer if she hides her nest and so she builds...

The tailorbird lives in southern China, India, and Southeast Asia, and the female usually nests in a garden or on cultivated land. She chooses one or two large, living leaves on a tree and draws their edges together, using her beak and feet. She makes small holes down the sides with the sharp point of her beak. Then she twists spiders' webs, bark, and plant fibers into threads and pushes them through the holes to hold the leaves together. Each stitch is fastened with a rough knot. Inside this leafy pocket the tailorbird can build her nest of grasses, plant down, and fibers — safely camouflaged among the trees.

Bowl-and-doily spiders need to trap their food and so they build...

The little bowl-and-doily spider is found in North America and has relatives, known as sheet-web or hammock-web spiders, in many parts of the world. Its name derives from the fact that it spins two webs, the upper one shaped like a shallow bowl, the lower one like a flat doily.

When an insect gets entangled in the bowl, the spider bites through the web from below, pulls the insect through, and wraps it up. The two webs, as well as being an effective food trap, help to protect the spiders, who often hang between the bowl and the doily.

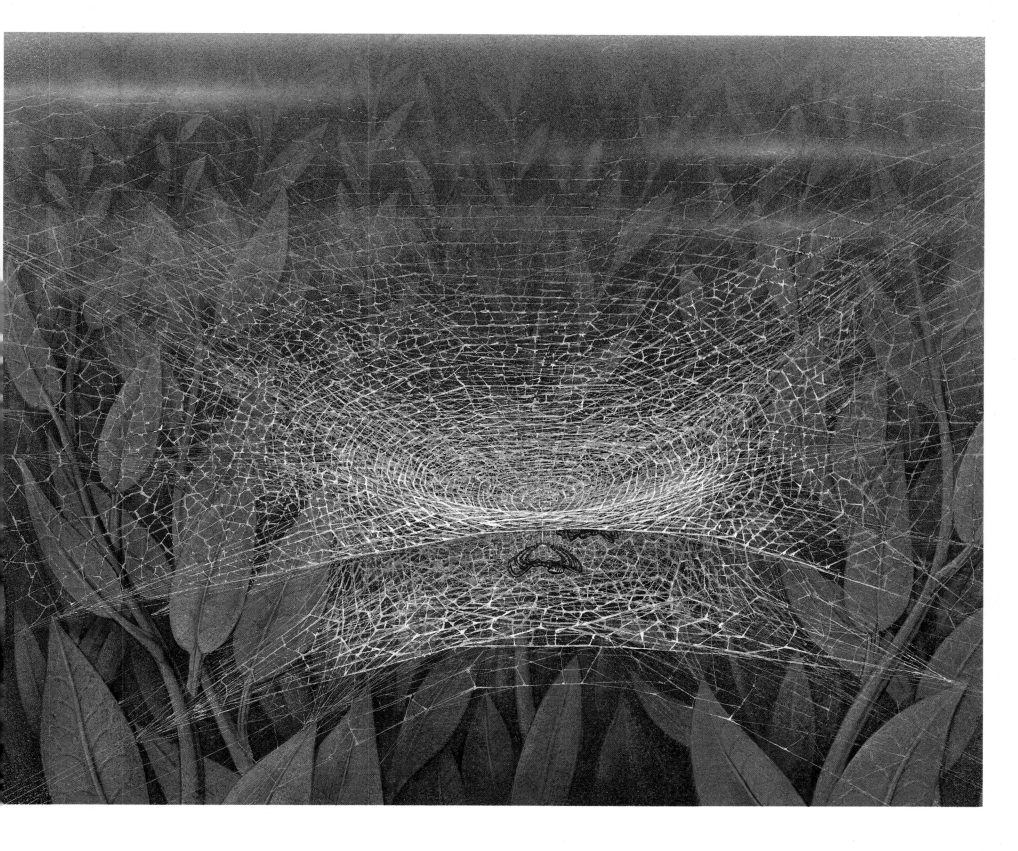

For a gladiator tree frog it's spawning time and so he builds...

The gladiator tree frog comes from South America.
It spends most of the year up in the trees, but moves down
to the ground during spawning time.
At the edge of a pond or slow-moving stream the male frog
builds a round enclosure out of clay, smoothing the walls with
his spatula-like fingers.
A few days later, when he's finished, he sits inside and calls out
for a mate. He will drive away all males, but any female he attracts
will inspect his enclosure before joining him to spawn.
Their tadpoles will be well protected from predators in their
walled nursery. While they grow, water will be seeping in,
raising the level inside until the time when they're ready
to swim over the walls and out into the wider world.

A three-spined stickleback always protects his eggs and so he builds...

The three-spined stickleback is found in ponds, slow-flowing streams, and sometimes even pools along the seashore.

During the mating season, the male chooses a shallow, weedy place. He makes a small dip in the bed of the stream with his snout and fills it with vegetation, mixing it with a gluey secretion from his kidneys so that it sticks together in a loose ball. Then he pushes through it to form a tunnel.

When a female approaches, he performs a kind of courtship dance, to which she eventually responds by swimming into his nest so that her head and tail stick out at either end. In this position she lays some of her eggs.

A successful male attracts several females to lay eggs in his nest. Once he has fertilized the eggs, he guards them for about ten days until they hatch, and continues to care for the tiny fish for some time afterward.

A caddis-fly larva is soft and vulnerable and so it builds...

The adult caddis fly lives around streams and rivers throughout the world. The female lays her eggs in water. As soon as a larva hatches from its egg it begins to secrete a sticky silk thread from a gland near its mouth and winds it around its body. Then it presses itself onto nearby objects such as small shells, stones, and grains of sand, which stick to the silk to form a hard, protective, well-camouflaged case, which is much smaller than a person's little finger. The case is open at both ends, allowing water to flow through so that the larva can breathe.

The larva lives inside the case for about a year, adding to it as it grows. When it is ready to emerge, it bites its way out with its strong jaws, floats to the water's surface, and takes to the air as a caddis fly.

Beavers seek a safe home for their family... and so they build.

Beavers live in North America, Europe, and northern Asia, and are famous for their building skills.

They use sticks, stones, and roots to build a dam across a slow-moving stream or river, filling in the gaps with finer vegetation, reeds, and mud or clay to make it watertight.

The structure may also be anchored downstream with tree trunks and boulders.

The dam creates an artificial lake within which the beavers can build their lodge — a cone-shaped woodpile hollowed out to form a living chamber with one or more underwater tunnels leading into it.

The walls are lined with mud, and the roof left more loosely built to let in air.

A whole beaver family will live in the lodge, safely protected from predators.